A PUP'S PRACTICAL GUIDE TO
UNDERSTANDING AND MANAGING ANXIETY

By Izzy Dog & Friends

Izzy illustrations by Emma Judson; Milo, Dylan, Zola illustrations Phil McCormick; pictures of Izzy (p.4) and Teya (p.5) by Graham Fisher; Dylan illustration on page 30 by Laura O'Connell; all other illustrations + page 13 and 39 iStock.

Page design by Cara Thurlbourn

Photo credits: Author's own.

ISBN: 978-1-9162533-1-5

CONTENTS

You can follow us on Facebook to keep in touch.

www.thek9project.co.uk

FOREWORD

"Dogs make such a difference to our lives. They offer companionship, make us laugh, get us outside, and can give us a reason to get up in the morning. We know dogs can help alleviate anxiety and depression in people, but often forget that many dogs also have these emotions too.

Drawing on the experiences of the ex-homeless dogs of the K9 Project, this book provides an insight into what we can learn from our canine companions. This includes some important life lessons on the benefits of movement, the importance of sleep, relaxation, sharing of feelings and learning to focus. Presented in a fun way with activities and colour photos, Chris Kent opens the door to conversations about worry and anxiety."

Dr Daniel Allen

Animal Geographer

Lecturer and Programme Director for Geography, Keele University

Founder of Pet Theft Reform campaign.

'Special Recognition' Award - Daily Mirror's People's Pet Awards 2021.

Nominated for the 'Petition Campaign of the Year Award' at the Your UK Parliament Awards 2022.

FOREWORD

Anxiety problems in young people were already on the rise before the pandemic hit. Since then, cases have risen dramatically. Not surprising given the uncertainty and constant changes in what we can and can't do. Young people have been isolated from their friends and expected to get on with schoolwork at home online. They will have watched more news than ever before and heard all the scary figures about how many people have died from this new virus. They will probably have seen their parents concerned and, possibly, affected financially. They might also have worried about passing the virus to vulnerable relatives.

Those of us working with dogs to support people know just how helpful they can be with their lack of judgement, total acceptance, and openness.

In this book, the dogs share their wisdom and experience so that people of all ages (whether they have a dog or not) can learn practical skills to manage and reduce their anxiety.

All shared in their unique inimitable way, of course!

Carrie Bates

Canine Assisted Therapist

AAT Dip

Dog Behaviour Practitioner IMDT/IMDTB

https://www.amindfulpaws.org/

Hi!

My name is Izzy. I expect you've noticed I am a dog? A pretty smart dog! This is my second book, and this time I am getting some help from my K9 Project dog crew. You can meet them later.

We are all dogs that have previously been homeless, abandoned, left to roam, or not looked after well. That means we can be in a good place to help young people, which is what we do for our day jobs, along with our humans. So, we are writing this in our spare time instead of sleeping on the sofa or chewing someone's socks.

You might ask why are we writing this?

We have noticed that many of the young people we work alongside experience something called ANXIETY. Since early 2020, we think that has got worse partly due to something called COVID. Us dogs do not really understand it, but it has meant that life is not quite the same, and we do notice that!

Because we are helpful dogs, we thought we'd try to write something that supports you by talking about some of the things we do that helps us.

Of course, we are all different and worry about different things, and different things may help us, so that's why we are all joining in and writing things!! There's space for you to write or draw your own things in as well.

We hope you find our little dogs' guide helpful...

Let us know!

Izzy x

INTRODUCTION

Firstly thank you so much for taking the time to check out our activity book, *You, Me and Anxiety*. This is the third book about the work of the K9 Project dogs, coming hot on the heels of *You Me and ADHD*, and a few years after Hounds Who Heal.

This time we focus on anxiety, currently a subject very much in the forefront of many peoples' minds, but in particular those of children and young people. Anxiety can be an issue for many of us when we are growing up, currently magnified by the changes we are all living through due to the Covid 19 virus and other world events.

Here at the K9 Project, we have seen an increase in both the number of young people experiencing anxiety and the levels for each individual. This is something borne out by colleagues in other education, health and care settings.

This book is our offering based on our years of working with children and young people and an understanding of current research. We will explain the differences between worry and anxiety, and provide some activities and exercises that we hope will help to increase understanding and alleviate stress.

I spend my weeks working alongside my amazing canine team of dogs who all have a back story, who have all been previously homeless, mistreated, neglected, and abandoned. They have every reason to lose faith and trust, and to avoid situations that can make them scared or worried. Instead they go out and live their best lives, and in doing so help young people to face their own worries and concerns, and to live their best lives in return.

This book is really a glimpse into what happens in some of our "live" sessions.

We hope that this transfers to the written page, and the activities, pictures, information and cute photos of dogs capture your attention and help you think about things in a slightly different way.

We also hope it will give those of you who have your own family dogs some ideas about how to adopt new approaches utilising your dog's natural abilities to be a de-stressor for your children.

Elsewhere, we thank all the contributors who have helped in a myriad of ways to make this book become a reality. We have been really fortunate to have some really helpful contributions from young people, parents and professionals.

In particular I need to thank my beautiful K9 Team (extra biscuits!) and the amazing young people who work alongside us each and every day, and who work so hard to overcome their challenges.

 What this book *is* and is *not* 

This book is *not* intended to be a complete guide to understanding and managing anxiety. It would be helpful to check out the organisations who offer support in this subject listed at the back of the book. These organisations offer a wider context and have a different range of expertise than we do. Their resources are excellent, please make use of them.

This book is *not* a substitute for medical advice and guidance, please do seek specialist advice if you need to or if you have additional concerns.

This book *may not* be helpful if you do not like dogs!

This book is *not* intended to be solely for SEND Children – however, many of the activities and discussions are very appropriate.

This book *is* a different way of talking about, exploring and learning about anxiety.

This book *is* intended to be used as a resource for parents, carers and education staff from a variety of settings, as well as for older children to look at themselves – whatever works for you.

This book *is* intended to "normalise" some aspects of worry and anxiety, to reduce stress and to remind us that we are definitely "not alone".

This book *is* intended to open the door to difficult conversations, using the non-judgemental and friendly voices of a group of rescue dogs.

Chris Kent, K9 Project Founder and Lead

MEET THE GANG

Izzydog

Hi I'm Izzy! I am pretty confident about many things but the things that make me anxious are meeting new dogs I do not know and trying to make friends. I also get anxious if I have to go without food. Things that help me with my anxiety are kind people and extra dinners.

I have been helped to write this book by my k9 dog friends - you can meet them next.

Teya and Dylan

We both come from Cyprus. We were not looked after well and we got very thin, sick and sad. We lived out on mountains and fields and tried to look after ourselves, before some people came and "rescued" us. Once we were healthy we came to live in England. We both like cuddles, running, dinner and sleeping on a comfy sofa. Things that make us anxious are loud noises, people shouting and getting angry, and sometimes Teya worries about whether she is doing the right thing. We are both helped with our anxiety by people being kind, being allowed to learn at out own pace and being with each other.

Milo and Zola, also known as Little and Large

We both come from Romania. We were born in fields there and lived on mice and other small creatures. It was very cold. We did not know each other in Romania but were rescued from the fields and then came to live in England with the K9 Crew. Things we like are hunting for mice, chasing birds, running and cuddles. Milo (Large)is worried about tall men, sticks, brooms or loud noises, and people coming up behind him. Zola (Little) is not frightened of anything much but does not like car rides. We are helped with our fears by people being kind and by learning to do new things, but slowly.

WHAT IS ANXIETY ?

What are we really talking about ?

The humans helped with this bit, as did many young people who we know and see each week.

"A FEELING OF WORRY, NERVOUSNESS, OR UNEASE ABOUT SOMETHING WITH AN UNCERTAIN OUTCOME." (THE OXFORD DICTIONARY)

Anxiety is a natural human response and is the brain's alarm bell – a way of letting us know when there is something we need to take notice of. It is also a way of keeping us safe. Although anxiety is a normal human reaction, it can creep up and take over our lives. This is not good.

What is the difference between worry and anxiety?

Worry tends to stay in our mind

Anxiety affects both body and mind.

Worry is specific

Anxiety is more generalised.

Worry is grounded in reality

Anxiety can be about imaginary things (catastrophic thinking).

Worry is temporary

Anxiety is long-standing.

Worry doesn't impair function

Anxiety does.[1]

Let's go into some more detail...

Worry tends to be logical – about a definite thing. Your brain is trying to make sense of a threat and to problem-solve a solution. Once you have solved that problem the worry goes away, and you have learned that you can manage it. This can build your confidence and sense of control, which is a good thing.

Anxiety creeps in and can affect your ability to function (that means to do normal, everyday things). You may have trouble sleeping and your memory may be affected. You may get a lot of physical symptoms such as feeling sick, trembly or faint, and a fast heart beat. This means your problem solving skills get fuzzy and you lose confidence and have trouble finding a way through, which in turn means you can feel like things are beyond your control. Generalised anxiety (which is where those feelings are about everything and anything ALL of the time) is harder to solve as it is vague. It takes more work to change the pattern that your brain has learned.

Generalised anxiety can affect everything you do, even when you actually enjoy doing it. This can make life very difficult and not fun!!

All of us dogs are lucky really as the part of the brain that makes us anxious (the pre-frontal cortex) is much smaller in dogs' brains than in humans. The pre-frontal cortex is the part of the brain that helps humans plan things, work towards goals, work out the consequences of actions, control behaviour and imagine consequences, work out what is good vs bad, and predict outcomes.

This can sometimes mean that human brains are very BUSY. And can worry about lots of things all at the same time.

This part of the brain is still developing until humans are in their 20's, so as a child or young person it sometimes gets a bit muddled.

The pre-frontal cortex is smaller in dogs, so you can see why we cannot do all those things as well as humans (which is why we often end up in trouble in the human world as we are impulsive and cannot always think about the consequences of our actions!)

However, the really good thing about it is that we do not OVER THINK things. Which humans seem to do a lot of. Although we can experience joy, or fear, or worry, we do it "in the moment". Whereas humans can "imagine" things to be anxious about in the future or in the past. Humans are good at worrying about things that may never even happen.

Dogs tend to worry about simple things...

Human worries are more complicated...

What do you worry about?

Have a think about your own worries and anxieties – you could write /draw them and see if they are worry or anxiety (or both); or discuss it with someone who might be helping you think about these things.

STRESS, ANXIETY AND FEAR

The really good thing is that some worry and anxiety is NOT ALL BAD.

Everyone gets worried and anxious sometimes – it is a healthy part of our bodies' responses to life!

It is the body and brain's way of prodding us to take some action, take notice of something, keep ourselves safe and spot danger. It is also a chance for us to practise our problem solving skills to make changes so we can reduce the anxiety.

However, too much anxiety can make you feel physically ill, have trouble sleeping and eating, and can become such a habit that you lose confidence. Sometimes everything we are asked to do puts us under pressure and then we get really STRESSED.

Think about the situations that cause you pressure.

Do other people put you under pressure?

Do you put yourself under pressure?

What helps you release that pressure?

Some stress can also be good, as most of us often need a little bit of pressure to get us to do things (like get out of bed in the morning or revise for a test).

NATASHA'S DEFINITION OF STRESS:

"IT'S LIKE BEING ON A TRAIN AND THE CARRIAGE IS ALREADY PRETTY FULL. THEN YOU STOP AT A STATION AND MORE PEOPLE GET ON. NO-ONE GETS OFF. THEN YOU TRAVEL A BIT MORE AND STOP, AND EVEN MORE PEOPLE GET ON. THE DOORS CLOSE AND THERE'S NOWHERE FOR YOU TO GO. THIS KEEPS HAPPENING OVER AND OVER AND EVENTUALLY YOU FEEL LIKE THE TRAIN WILL EXPLODE."

And then there is FEAR.

"An unpleasant emotion caused by the threat or perceived threat of danger, pain, or harm."

We can feel FEAR about real things or things we imagine- the brain cannot tell the difference. Some people quite like being scared or fearful for a while (have you ever watched a horror film or do you know anyone who does?). However, fear in the long term can also be tiring and affect our emotional wellbeing.

BRAIN STUFF!

Zola says: This is complicated – way too hard for us dogs to understand, so the human wrote it. This bit is for young adults to read themselves or for parents to understand the process and maybe help if the children are very young.

The brain is an amazing thing. It receives thousands of pieces of information each and every second, through all of our five senses.

In order to stop it overloading, it filters the information by deleting, distorting or generalising. This means it can focus on the things it considers to be important.

Each one of us deletes, distorts and generalises things differently depending on our past life experience, memories, beliefs and values, and our current emotional and physical state.

Because it likes to work in patterns, and it likes to be right, it is hard to develop a pattern of thinking that is different to your usual thinking pattern.

This means, for instance, if you have had bad experiences at school and expect school to always be bad, your brain will filter out or distort the information that disagrees with that – even if you have a good teacher who you like or good experiences. Equally, if you have low self confidence and your self talk is around being "rubbish" at everything, your brain will ignore all the messages it receives where it is obvious you are good at many things.

By working in these patterns, the brain develops "neural pathways" – the more we use these pathways the quicker the processing gets – so some will be a bit like a motorway and some, if we do not use them, will be like a winding country lane.

The good news is that even if your brain is hardwired for anxiety, this can be changed. But guess what? Like anything, it needs to be worked at!!

The brain is described as having "plasticity" which means we can change those "neural pathways". Science says that it takes around 66 days (sometimes more) to form a new habit. The longer you have been thinking in a certain pattern, the longer it may take to change it. But it can be done.

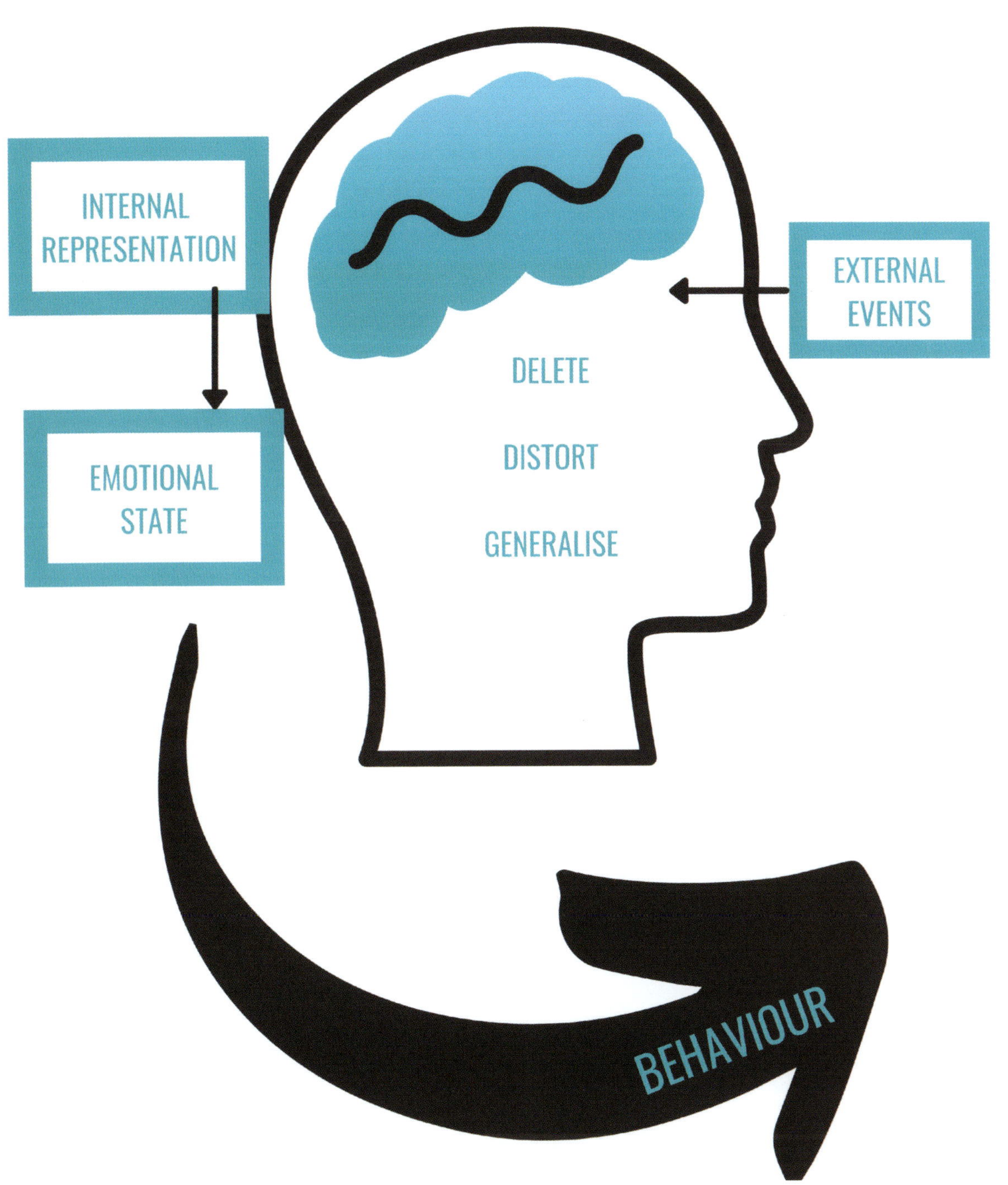
INTERNAL REPRESENTATION
EMOTIONAL STATE
EXTERNAL EVENTS
DELETE
DISTORT
GENERALISE
BEHAVIOUR

LET'S TALK ABOUT COMFORT ZONES

Your Comfort Zone is a place where you feel completely safe and happy. A comfort zone can be a physical place (i.e. your room or under the stairs) or people (your family or friends) or it can be an activity (reading/listening to music).

Then we have your Stretch Zone. This is a place where you can do things, but they are hard, they are a s t r e t c h. Things in your stretch zone may be meeting new people or going to new places. You can sometimes do things in the s t r e t c h zone for a short time, then you have to get back into your comfort zone otherwise you may end up in the Panic Zone.

We don't learn a lot in the PANIC ZONE, but learning and confidence building happens in the stretch zone.

The aim is to make your comfort zone as big as possible by moving things from your Stretch Zone into your Comfort Zone

This is how we build our confidence, learn problem solving skills and learn to live a fuller life.

We talk about this more when we get to the DO THE THING part later on!

COMFORT ZONE
PANIC ZONE
STRETCH ZONE

MILO'S COMFORT ZONES...

TALL MEN
NEW PEOPLE
BROOMS

NEW PLACES
NEW PEOPLE

HOME
PEOPLE I KNOW

FILL IN YOUR OWN COMFORT ZONES MAP...

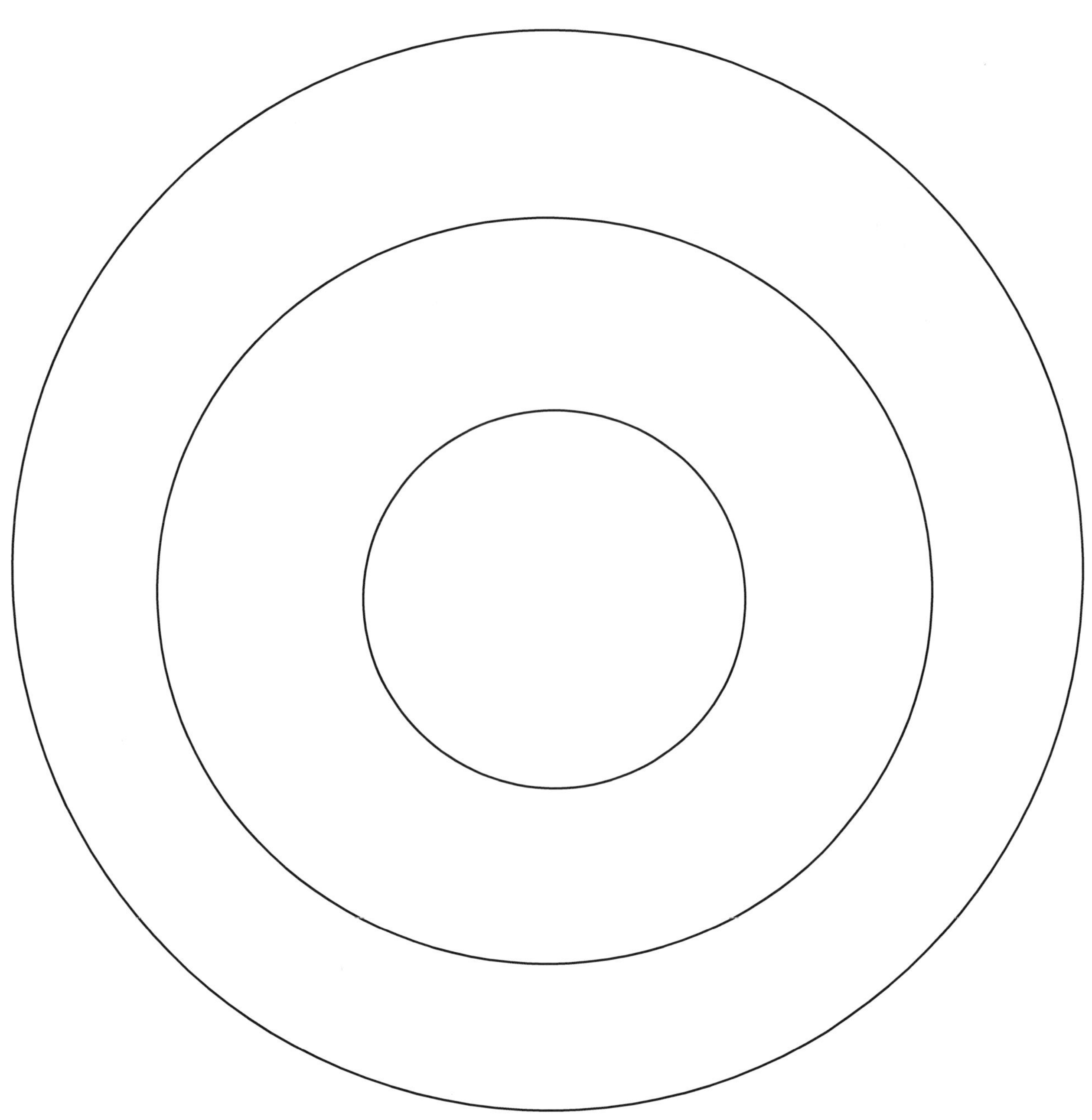

DO THE THING!

Milo here!

Go back and think about the Comfort Zone information. That thing you are worried about – the only way to change it is to face it, ONE SMALL STEP at a time, with support.

Being frightened of the broom means that whenever the humans sweep up our dog hair and the twigs we have chewed, it's scary for me and I have to go outside.

If a tall human comes in the house I have to run away and bark. If I am out for a walk and I see a tall human I get scared and don't enjoy the walk.

One way to solve this problem is for me to AVOID THE PROBLEMS – the human would never sweep up, we would never have visitors and I would never go out for a walk.

The downside of that is my world would be very small. Plus, I often like new people once I get to know them and I enjoy going out and sniffing new smells.

So we have to find a way to DO THE THING.

So with the broom we start with it standing in the kitchen – it's there all the time. I have forgotten all about it now when it is there, so it is now in my COMFORT ZONE when it is not moving. The humans notice I am happy with it and tell me I am a good boy. When they pick it up it goes back into my STRETCH ZONE. I'm now a bit uncomfortable with it. So they just pick it up for a little while, maybe move it a little bit, then they stand it still. It is back in my COMFORT ZONE. The next few times they move it, I do not notice, sometimes I get a treat or a pat on the head. Eventually after lots of REPETITIONS I am not scared of it. Mostly the broom is in my COMFORT ZONE even when it is moving. Sometimes it might still make me jump a bit, especially if a tall new person has been in the

house and I feel a bit overwhelmed, or if I woke up feeling a bit jittery. But mostly I do not mind the broom, and now my COMFORT ZONE has got a bit bigger.

We do similar things with tall men and going for walks and my COMFORT ZONE is getting LOTS bigger .

Things that help –

- Set your own goals so it is about things that are important to you.
- Work with people who understand you and will not rush you.
- Work with a dog if you can – that always helps.
- Remember some days you will find it harder than others. That is fine, and usual.
- Repetition – you have to keep doing the thing and practice lots.

Think about something in your stretch zone that you want to get more comfortable with and put in your comfort zone. Write down some ideas for what you could do to make this happen...

WHAT HELPS?

Now we know what anxiety is... is there anything we can do about it?

The good news is yes there is!

Make peace with anxiety

What does this mean?? Accept that it happens, anxiety is part of life.

We cannot avoid it if we go out and live a life.

We can learn to accept it but still challenge it, learn ways of changing our responses and grow beyond it.

All of us dogs do slightly different things to help us with our worries. It is important you try different things and work out what is right for you. You probably already have lots of things that can help you – here's some of ours!

Sometimes it can feel like no one can help and there is not a solution, it is important to remember that lots of people have anxiety and learn to make peace with it. You can too!

Think about what you'd say to a friend if they told you they were feeling anxious. Write down your reply in this box.

Teya says SLEEP!

Sleep allows our bodies and minds to rest and heal. It allows me to switch off and process things that have happened. I can sleep even if there is lots of noise. When I was in Cyprus and shut in small sheds with nothing to do, sleep helped me shut off from hunger and thirst. Although I am safe now, sleep is still very important to me... it helps if I have been running about lots so both my body and mind are tired.

I hear that sleep can be very hard for some humans – it is easy for most dogs.

Things that might help you are:

I know it's hard but turn off screens! Phones, computers... all of it! That light tricks your brain into thinking it's still daylight. Darkness can help or a really soft low light if you do not like the dark.

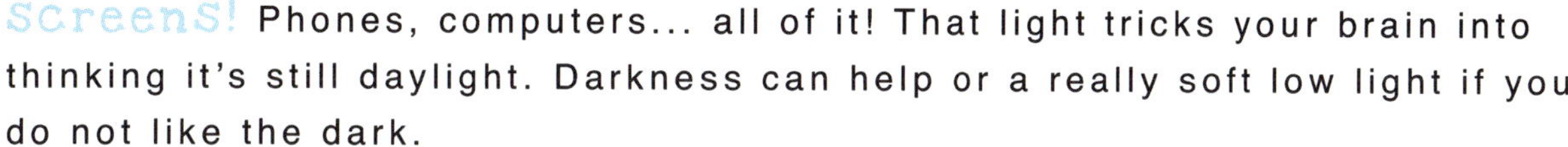

Curling up tight, use a heavy duvet/weighted blanket, sleeping next to your dog if allowed (or cat if you have to!) making sure you are not hungry or thirsty. Listening to calming music or meditations. Soothing smells like lavender.

Surrender to Sleep...

Write down your usual sleep pattern and then think about what changes you could make that might help you to sleep better. i.e. don't look at your phone or computer late at night!

Zola says speak up!

I like to BARK at things – if I am worried, or excited (sometimes I cannot tell the difference).

This usually feels really good at the time. I believe it is really important to let people know how you feel as soon as possible – worries can build up into a pattern and create generalised anxiety. The sooner you can get some support the better. I may not have words, but I am very good at letting people know what I want and when I want it. Of course, I do not always get it (sometimes humans can be a bit slow) so I have to keep on barking. Sometimes I can also sing in a lovely high pitched voice (the humans call that whining but I am not sure what that means). If that fails I might gently tap people with my paw or gaze into their eyes until they ask me what I want.

Think about the people you can go to for support or who you can share your worries with.

Does this help? If so, how? Are there any other ways this person/these people can help you?

Izzy says move!

The best thing that helps me is to MOVE – I like to run, jump, roll, stretch. I am really happy when I am moving, and if something (like another dog coming along) worries me then I keep moving and go straight past them.

When we get worried both dogs and humans can "freeze" and stand still. This allows the tension to build up inside us. If you feel that tension building up in your body, my advice is to remember to MOVE.

I doubt you humans can do all the fancy moves that I can. Maybe, instead you could wiggle your ankles, shake your shoulders, waggle your wrists, move your body, dance if you can, walk (preferably with a dog) or learn a new skill like a martial art or a sport. If any part of your body feels tense SHAKE IT OFF, or yawn, or move your tongue – you may be surprised at the difference it makes!!

It is important that you do not keep still but KEEP MOVING, maybe have a mantra to repeat in your head in time as you move.

What kind of movement do you enjoy?
What might help you to feel more relaxed?

Dylan and Milo say distract and focus!

We like to find an activity that means we have to focus totally on it.

We like to distract ourselves by sniffing, weeing, digging and chewing.

Here's a really good hole we dug together!

It was great fun and while we did it we were totally focussed.

Okay, that works for us but maybe digging and sniffing does not work for you, so how about thinking about the things you do to distract yourself.

It may be drawing, writing, computer based activities, playing a musical instrument, singing, wordsearches, anything that distracts your mind in a positive way from OVER THINKING.

In this way, your mind gets to focus on something else which helps the anxiety get left behind

ALL OF US DOGS LIKE TO LIVE IN THE MOMENT

We live most of our lives like this. We are HERE NOW, in this minute, not thinking about being anywhere else or doing anything else, or tomorrow, or yesterday or next year.

Think about the distractions that work for you?

Are they positive distractions?

Can you think of any new ones you can try?

THE THING ABOUT DOGS...

WHATEVER WE ARE DOING, WE ARE DOING IT 100% .

Sleeping, running, playing with toys, digging, doing zoomies in the garden, eating, that's where we are.

WE USE OUR SENSES TO KEEP US HERE, NOW.

Humans can be a bit out of touch with their senses as they generally rely on words to communicate and to make sense of the world. Sometimes humans have sensory processing issues, which means that some of their senses can get easily overwhelmed.

We use all of our senses – smell (that's usually our favourite) hearing, sight, touch, and taste (usually second favourite). Using our senses can anchor us to the present moment. Here's one way you can do the same:

WHEN YOU FEEL YOUR MIND RACING OR GETTING OUT OF CONTROL - BE MORE LIKE A DOG! FOCUS ON:

Three things you can see.

Three things you can touch.

Three things you can hear.

Really focus and look, feel, and listen. If you practice this it can block out your overthinking, and calm your busy mind.

BE KIND

Being kind not only helps other people, but also makes the person who is being kind feel good too. Human researchers have found that being kind can make people happier, is good for the heart, slows down the ageing process, improves relationships and is catching.[4]

As dogs we like to help each other and it makes us feel good. Ways we help each other include being pillows, providing friendship and companionship to each other, playing nicely together (sometimes letting the other dog win!) and helping each other if one dog is scared of something.

In the wild we would look for food together, travel together, share food, and keep each other warm if it is cold.

We also like to help humans too and feel that this is part of who we are and what we do. It makes us feel good, so we keep doing it.

Ways we help people include sensing how they feel and giving them affection, making them laugh, putting our heads on their knees when they are sad, letting them make a fuss of us which slows down their heart rate and calms them down.

With training we can do so many other things too like help with the washing and shopping, help people who cannot see get out and about, sniff out illness and find dangerous things like bombs and guns.

Here at the K9 project we help lots of young people get outside when usually they stay home due to their anxiety. They practise talking to us, and other people out and about. We help them build their confidence, learn problem solving skills and have fun!

We also help young people who are scared of dogs not be so scared.

All of this makes us very happy.

Kindness does help and make us feel good. The smallest thing can make a big difference – sometimes even just a smile from a human can make our doggy hearts sing! (We can recognise facial expressions remember![5])

It can be difficult if you are shy and worry about doing the wrong thing. Most people are kind inside, sometimes it can be hard to let it shine outside too! If you are trying to help someone else, then this makes you feel good, and can also take your mind away from your own worries too for a little while.

ACTIVITY

Maybe for the next few weeks you can have a think about how you can be kind to other people, perhaps your family to start.

Write down some things you could try to do remember they only have to be small things.

RELAXATION

One of the things that happens to our brain when we are anxious a lot is that it becomes hardwired for anxiety. This means that anxiety is our DEFAULT setting, and the place where our brain can go to really really quickly. We get better at things we practise a lot right? So it makes sense that if we practice being anxious then our brain gets really good at it and we have to work really hard to change it. Not that we intend to practise being anxious, but it becomes our default setting.

One way of doing this is to practise being relaxed. Sometimes humans are never relaxed they are so anxious all the time it stops them totally relaxing.

So, what do we mean by relaxation? The official definition is “the state of being free from tension and anxiety.”

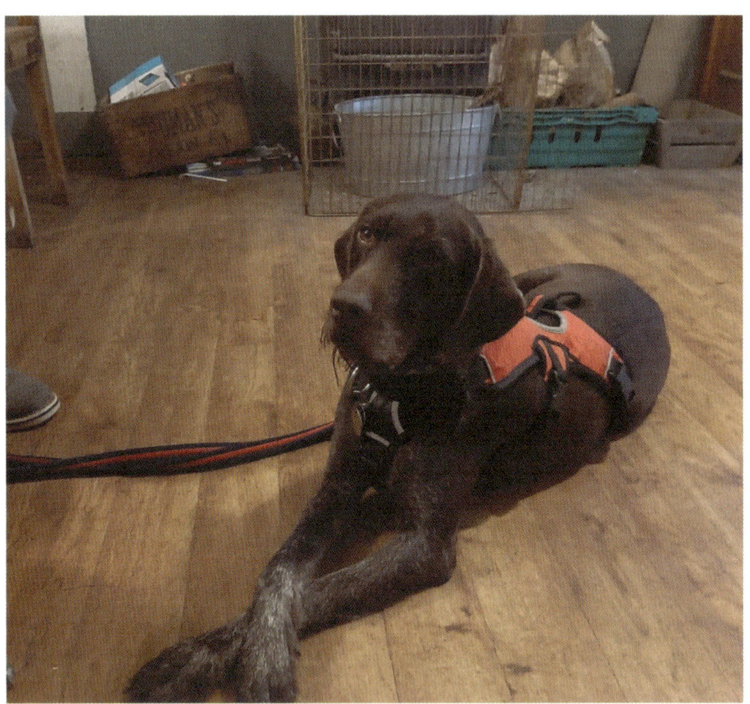

A bit like Dylan in this picture.

Relaxation is different to sleep. As Teya has already said, sleep is blissful and she has explained why it is very important to try and make the most of sleep.

Relaxation means you are chilled. You could be doing nothing or doing something, but you are FREE from tension and anxiety.

Dogs are good at this; in much the same way that they can abandon themselves to sleep, they can also abandon themselves to relaxation. Especially in warm sun, on comfy sofas or in front of the fire on cold winter's night.

There is nothing more calming than being with a group of dogs who are totally relaxed, breathing slowly and deeply. This can help us relax too, in the same way that stroking a dog (or cat) can.

So that's the good news. The bad news is that relaxation, if you haven't practised doing it, can be hard.

Guess what? You need to PRACTISE. You may have been practising (unintentionally) being anxious for a long time .

ACTIVITY

We need to experience being relaxed regularly so it is important to practise for really short periods of time to start with.

There are lots of things that can help to relax, lots of visual and audio meditations, guided visualisations, things to help to use your imagination in a positive way, listening to music that soothes you.

It is important to slow down, not rush, and breathe tension out of your body.

A good way to start is to practise breathing gently into your stomach, sitting still, being comfortable, for a few minutes at a time. This may feel strange at first, but this is where we have to keep going. Even five minutes a day will start to make a difference. There is a breathing exercise later in the book and some references at the end of the book to help.

There are other mindfulness activities in the book which may also help.

Appreciate relaxation- look for opportunities to relax, count it as a special time.

Practise

Relaxation can fill your body with good chemicals that can heal the damage constant anxiety can do to your system. Remember to CHILL .

MINDFULNESS

Phoebe & Chance

Here, our dog friends who work with Sam at Alternative Social Communication have given us some other activities to try when we get stressed or worried...

When we get anxious we might breathe shallowly and this causes our heart to race. The brain picks up on the increased heart rate due to lack of oxygen, thinks there is something wrong and switches from a calm intellectual state to an emotional state. This in turn leads to the fight, flight or freeze state of mind.

If our bodies do not get enough oxygen, the heart beats faster to increase the supply of oxygen to the brain. The brain realises that the reduced supply of oxygen is a threat to survival and so switches to fight, flight or freeze mode. This makes it impossible to think rationally or answer questions, particularly in exams/tests/interviews etc. The only way to get the brain to switch back to the intellectual state is to increase the oxygen supply to the brain by carrying out three rescue breaths.

You might have noticed that us dogs often breathe with our mouths open to increase the oxygen to our brain and because if we are hot we cannot sweat like people do (you may find you sweat when you are anxious too!)

You could do something like Rescue Breaths...

ACTIVITY

Sit up straight in your chair, close your eyes and your mouth.

Slowly breathe in through your nose. As you breathe in, concentrate on how it feels as it enters and travels through your nostrils. Is it warm? Is it cold? Can you feel your lungs inflate? You should be able to feel your tummy rise and fall – you need to breathe deeply enough for the air to travel below your chest.

Pause for a second and then release the breath. As it leaves your body can you feel your tummy fall, is the air warmer or is it colder? Feel all of it pass back out through your nostrils before repeating.

Repeat this three times and then your body will have re-oxygenated and your heart rate will return to normal, allowing your brain to switch back to a calm state.

If you can stroke a dog once calm, this is even better.

Once you get used to breathing in this way you can try doing it anywhere. The key is that you need to breathe through your nose. You could try counting in 1,2,3 and out 1,2,3,4. And remember to breathe SLOWLY a bit like dogs do when we are resting and relaxed.

Another thing to try is rubbing the bottom of your ear lobes. We have lots of nerve endings in our ears – people and dogs alike – that release feel good chemicals called endorphins.This can also calm us down.

Us dogs like to play with toys to burn off excess energy and they can help you too. You can get stress toys just for people – warning we may like them too!! It is worth using things around us. One of the best might be a rock or stone from the garden or beach. Hold in your hands and gently explore it with your fingertips.

Ask yourself the following things:

How does it feel? Hot or cold? Smooth or rough? What is the texture like? Is it heavy or light? Does it remind you of anything?

Now close your eyes and ask the same questions.

These are also distraction techniques that get our brains thinking about something other than what is making us anxious.

This can be very helpful.

PHOEBE

CHANCE

A MINDFUL WALK
(HOPEFULLY WITH A DOG)

Our friends Barnaby and Leo have helped with this one – they work with Carrie at A Mindful Paws.

Dogs like to go out and run about. When we do, we use all of our senses; it just comes naturally for us. Humans have to work harder at it!! This is really called mindfulness. Here's a way for you to practise it!

• As you step out of your door, take a deep breath and smell the air.

• Notice the warmth of the sun or the crispness of the breeze on your face.

• As you take your first steps, feel your feet landing on the ground.

• If you have a dog, can you feel the lead in your hand? What is the texture like? How much tension is there?

• Notice how your dog is sniffing as they go; they are taking in every moment.

• What can you hear as you walk? Birds? Traffic? People? Other dogs?

• Listen carefully and see how far away you can hear noise from.

• What can you see around you? Notice the hedgerows, gardens, verges, and trees. How are they individual?

• If you go to a park, field or woods, what is the ground like underfoot?

• Walk off the pathway and explore.

• Watch the squirrels running up the trees.

• Notice the shape of leaves on the trees.

• Look for patterns in nature- these are very calming

• Explore rabbit or fox holes if you or the dog finds them.

• Find somewhere to stop and sit.

• Take a deep breath, what can you smell?

• What can you feel?

- What can you see?
- What can you hear?
- After a few moments of just sitting and observing, take a deep breath, stand up and make your way home

MIND FULL OR MINDFUL?

Think about things that you find relaxing and draw your own mindfulness cartoons in the box above.

REMEMBER

Every step forward is important and is starting to break your brain's patterns of being afraid and anxious. Don't rush this unless you feel ready too.

Remember there will be steps backwards sometimes too. That is okay, and normal, and happens to us all.

Because you experience worry and anxiety now, does not mean you will always have to.

What people think success looks like:

Walking in a straight line

But success and progress normally involve going sideways, backwards, and forwards.

Ups and downs

Think about how long you have been feeling anxiety. It will take some time to change that. The amazing thing is:

Once you start to make progress it builds and builds.

Practise talking to yourself in a kind way – give yourself the help and praise you would give your best friend if they needed it.

Check in with people who help you regularly.

Give yourself a little challenge and get into that stretch zone!

And remember:

- You are unique and amazing.
- You have a right to live your best life.
- You can do this.
- We believe in you!!
- Believe in yourself.

We all really really hope you have found this helpful.

Thank you for letting us dogs help you on your way to your best life.

We'd love for you to contact our human to let us know how you are doing.

Lots of love Izzydog, Teya Zola Milo and Dylan

ABOUT THE AUTHOR

Chris Kent is a multi skilled professional who has worked across the public, private and charitable sectors running her own successful training consultancy within social care as well as working in youth work, criminal justice, and education settings. She set up the K9 Project in 2008 linking her lifelong passions for working with people and animals to create a unique and inspirational project. The K9 Project has won awards for youth work, young people's participation, adult employability skills an business innovation. In addition Chris herself has won a National Animal Hero Award from the Peoples Pet Awards. Her qualifications and experience across diverse settings have enabled her to work creatively to support people experiencing life challenges, working alongside her team of ex homeless dogs.

For this book she has partnered with Izzydog, who was roaming the streets as a stray before being taken in by a shelter, then found by Chris, to provide an alternative way of thinking and talking about anxiety. They are ably assisted by the non judgemental voices of her other K9 Team members.

Please check out her K9 Project website for more information as well as the facebook pages.

www.thek9project.co.uk

https://www.facebook.com/IzzyDogBooks/

https://www.facebook.com/thek9project/

RESOURCES

References

Page 8. (1) John Devore MSW behavioural health social worker worker at Henry Ford Live Well Centre www.henryford.com

Page 10 (2) www.annablake.com

Page 14 (3) Lexicon Oxford Dictionary

Page 15 Comfort Zones Is a psychological/learning theory commonly adapted for use in human behaviour, and performance management , as well as some horse and dog training models. Hard to establish exactly who developed it (many claim to) but it derives from Yerkes Law developed in 1906. Lots of information available on the internet if you wish to learn more.

Page 28 (4) David Hamilton Why Kindness Is Good For You

Page 30 Brain Stuff is simplified version of the NLP Communication Model developed by Richard Bandler and John Grinder. It explains how we receive information that comes from the outside world, how we process it and how it influences the way we communicate/respond to others.

Resources and useful Organisations

Young Minds have informative and helpful information about anxiety and other difficulties young people may be facing. – suitable for young people to access. Information for young people, parents and professionals https://www.youngminds.org.uk

The Art of Meditation https://theartofmeditation.org

Not particularly good for very young, but for anyone interested in an online course about anxiety and ways to combat it including meditations, exercise and discussions for a reasonable cost it may be worth checking out their Anxiety Course.

A MindfulPaws https://www.amindfulpaws.org/

Cambridgeshire based support service for young people.

CASSIE https://www.alternativesocialcommunication.com/

Cambridgeshire based support/alternative education service for young people.

Your local Child and Adolescent Mental Health Services (CAMHS) are a useful source of local info.

Our very good friends at **Love Learning from dogs** can be found at (for all things resilience based and much, much, more.)

https://lovelearningfromdogs.com/

Some young people find Apps very helpful – here are a couple

SAM Self Help for Anxiety Management

Headspace

Calm

And finally, here's a mention for our friend Phil, who did the drawings of the dogs... here is his merchandise shop:

https://www.redbubble.com/people/Dracholos/shop?utm_source=rb-native-app&utm_campaign=share-artist&utm_medium=android&fbclid=IwAR3Ts8dLPhRiArcx_I4ZF4LYRkvuIYtA2g9t74t7nSLRBDoGx26BKxHBo5Y

Printed in Great Britain
by Amazon